COMFORT FOOD
FOR
AN UNCOMFORTABLE
STOMACH

BY A KID FOR KIDS

JOSH COHEN

Contents

Dedication

I would like to dedicate this book to my fabulous mother, Lisa, who has taught me how to cook along with many other important life long skills. Around 10 years ago during the holiday season, my mom gave me a KitchenAid mixing bowl. I was very disappointed to receive this gift, in my mind, it was a lame gift. This same holiday, my older brother received a cool Star Wars lightsaber. I would later understand the importance of cooking and the value of this very thoughtful gift that has lasted for years, used hundreds of times, while the lightsaber my brother received was broken in a couple weeks. My mother understood the value of teaching and the lifelong importance of eating what you enjoy while still enjoying what you eat. Thank you so much for all your support over the years for your continued dedication to our family!

Love,
Josh

Forward

I am a 17 year-old high school student living in Orange County, California. I am not an expert at Irritable Bowel Disease, Health or Nutrition. I am just a kid trying to help other kids who suffer from these diseases that make it harder to enjoy food and activities that I used to take for granted. I wanted to share some of the adjustments that I was able to make in my diet that allowed me to feel like I wasn't missing out.

I always had a sensitive stomach. When I was 13 years-old, I went on an amazing trip to Cooperstown, New York for a baseball tournament, and my stomach was just not right and we didn't know why. Two years later, I ended up in the emergency room with what my doctor thought was a possible appendicitis. After we realized that this was not the problem, I had a colonoscopy and was diagnosed with a form of ulcerative colitis. It shouldn't have been a big surprise, as my mom has a mild form of the disease, but we were still shocked. I am on medication now, but I clearly find that what I put in my body has a huge impact on how I feel. Simple changes like limiting dairy, avoiding fried foods and adjusting recipes by switching to almond flour instead of wheat flour can make a serious improvement in my health.

Over the past few years, I've gathered my favorite recipes that don't bother my digestive system and assembled them into this book. I developed this book because I wanted to share my favorite recipes with others who might be having a tough time to find food they enjoy while still living a healthy lifestyle. Also, many of the recipes I feature in this book can be enjoyed by the entire family. I am constantly learning about healthy food options from various sources and, as I write this book, I am taking a college class on nutrition.

These recipes and suggestions work for me, and I hope that some of them work for you or your child and can empower all struggling with Irritable Bowel Disease.

Great Healthy Food Brands I Enjoy

I have found a number of manufacturers that offer products that have clean ingredients that agree with my stomach:

1) *Simple Mills* is a Chicago-based company founded by a woman who wanted healthier foods and found nothing great on the market, so she decided to make these foods herself. They make a yummy farmhouse cheddar cracker that tastes like a "Cheez-It". Also they have premade baking mixes that taste really good.

2) *Siete* is an Austin, Texas-based company that makes healthy, simple mexican food necessities such as tortilla's, tortilla chips, sauces and dips. They use quality ingredients and don't use the nasty filler conventional products use. I have eaten their tortilla chips and can attest to their great taste and robust flavor. They have options available for any consumer who enjoys authentic mexican cuisine while still being a healthier alternative. Also, I relate with this company as the founder was diagnosed with multiple autoimmune issues and wanted to still eat great tasting food. Inspired by this company, the goal of my cookbook is to empower others to enjoy what they eat and feel good.

3) *Coconut Bliss* is a dessert company based in Eugene, Oregon that uses all USDA organic ingredients that make spectacular dairy free ice cream. Coconut Bliss uses high quality ingredients that taste fresh and real unlike some other cheap brands that are filled with chemicals. Particularly in my family, filled with ice cream lovers, we stock up with the necessary

products which go into my peanut butter smoothie (page 60) or are a tasty snack whenever anybody needs to fulfill their sweet tooth.

4) *Califia* is a California based company that makes delicious plant based beverages including coconut milk, almond milk, coffee, coffee creamer, yogurt and juice. My family mainly enjoys their coconut almond milk and chocolate coconut almond milk. Before we knew about Califia's different milks, we would buy the small coffee creamer bottles and drink that like regular milk because it tasted silky, sweet and incredibly delicious. However, my father wasn't very happy with buying such small amounts and paying the price for the small quantity, so when we came across the flavored milk, we began to fall in love with the coconut almond milks and now only drink Califia coconut almond milk. The coconut almond milk is a refrigerator staple as it can be used in many recipes such as the peanut butter smoothie (see page 60).

5) *Cybele's* vegetable pasta superfood and brown rice pasta are amazing pantry staples that are an excellent pasta option disguised as a vegetable. If I only have vegetable pasta, it bothers my stomach. If I combine it with brown rice pasta, my stomach does great. This is because the vegetable pasta is filled with fiber and protein along with many other nutritional benefits, while tasting similar to regular pasta.

6) *Applegate* is a natural and organic meat producer that focuses on providing quality, sustainable meat production. All of Applegates products are antibiotic free, humanely raised and use non-GMO ingredients. I love their chicken nuggets as they bring me back to my childhood. They also make great chicken sausage. These procedures are very important as many diseases spread through animals and sustainable meat production limits the likelihood of these viruses spreading. Watch this very interesting video by Nas Daily and you will understand why this is important: https://youtu.be/VGki7hc1CZI

Natural and Alternative Sweeteners and Oils

Sweeteners

What's bad about regular cane sugar, sugar in the raw and/or organic cane sugar? These sugars destroy the good gut bacteria which suppresses your immune system. They also lead to obesity and heart disease. The common sugar also has no protein, essential fats, vitamins or minerals, it harms metabolism, and can even be addictive. Now more than ever, there are sugar substitutes on the market that are healthier, natural and even provide health benefits.

Monk fruit is a very popular sweetener that doesn't taste bitter or metallic, it is 300 times sweeter than sugar. There are also many monk fruit blends which are 1:1, meaning one cup of the monk fruit blent is equal to one cup of cane sugar.

Stevia is another sugar that is a natural plant, a sweet leaf from South America. ¾ teaspoons stevia=2 tsp sugar, hard to bake with, but is great because it comes in both liquid and powder form. Another positive is because both Stevia and monk fruit are 0 on the glycemic index and don't spike your blood sugar like common sugar.

Coconut palm sugar is a nutrient dense sweetener, low glycemic, made from the sap from the coconut, which is rich in iron, zinc and is good for your gut.

Real Maple syrup has a great flavor and is low on the glycemic index and is loaded with tons of nutrients and nutritionally dense

Honey is a great option, but you shouldn't buy pasteurized honey because it kills a lot of the nutrients of the honey. However, raw honey has more nutrients and vitamins. Also, I suggest watching the documentary "Rotten" which explains how companies in China manipulate the honey, which is why it is important to know where your honey is sourced from. (best deal at Costco)

Erythritol is a low calorie sugar alcohol that is a common sweet substitute for sugar. Erythritol is superior to other sugar alcohols as it gets absorbed into the bloodstream and 90% of it gets excreted through the body. Erythritol has been known to cause stomach aches in high amounts, but is fine in small amounts. For me, I feel fine after consuming Erythritol when I have a couple cookies. In fact, my favorite erythritol product is Lily's Dark Chocolate Chips which tastes very similar to real chocolate with simple ingredients.

Oils

Please note it is good to buy an oil that is expeller pressed, which refers to the process in which the oil is extracted from the raw material from a machine(as seen below). The reason this method is good is because it doesn't use any chemicals in the process. The process also occurs at a relatively low temperature (a range of 140°–210° F) which keeps the nutrients and other benefits intact, unlike other methods of extracting oil.

Avocado Oil:
A great oil to replace canola oil and doesn't add any flavor. It has a high smoke point (520° F) which makes it great for cooking with high heat, on a grill or making a stir fry. What's good about avocado oil is that it is filled with omega 9's, which helps reinforce omega 3's. Avocado oil and olive oil both have oleic acids which is a fatty acid that is great for the health of your body. Avocado oil is a very versatile oil that reduces cholesterol, improves heart health, features lutin that is an antioxidant that benefits eye health, may reduce the pain and

stiffness associated with osteoarthritis and improves the appearance of your skin. (good price at Costco)

Olive Oil

Olive oil is rich in monounsaturated oleic acid. This fatty acid is believed to have many beneficial effects and is a healthy choice for cooking. Furthermore, oleic acid has been linked to reducing inflammation. Olive oil is not known to increase weight and is filled with antioxidants and vitamins E and K. Olive oil is also a great cooking oil as it has a burning temperature at 410° F.

Coconut Oil (virgin)

Coconut oil is a very misunderstood oil. Initially dietitians believed that coconut oil was harmful, however, the studies involved refined coconut oil. Refined means that the oil may have been heated, bleached, and/or deodorized. This process strips the oil of over 80% of its healthy disease-fighting polyphenols and generates cell-toxic hydrogen.

Virgin coconut oil has not been harmfully treated with heat or chemicals; this means it contains about seven times more healthy polyphenols as does refined coconut oil. Additionally, according to two January 2020 studies published by The Journal of Mechanisms of Ageing and Development found that using virgin coconut oil reported significant elevations in 'good' HDL cholesterol and no changes in 'bad' LDL cholesterol.

Why canola oil is bad:

Because it is a processed and refined oil that changes the fatty acid from a polyunsaturated fat to a hydrogenated fat which uses a chemical called hexane which excretes the oil which is not good for you. Hydrogenated trans fats are difficult for many people, especially those with digestive issues, because it takes the body 51 days to break down the CIS bonds, putting a lot of pressure on the digestive system.

Natural Flavors

What are natural flavors?

Natural flavors are used to increase that taste of food. In order to be natural, the flavor needs to start off with a natural ingredient such as a fruit and then chemicals can be added, making it not natural. The purpose of this strategy is to take the natural ingredient and then copy it in a lab and then improve on it to make it more addictive. These companies that make these flavors purposely make these "natural" flavors begin with a burst of energy and then end with a taste that doesn't linger, causing the consumer to eat more of their product. In my opinion, this is one of the biggest lies in the supermarket as these natural flavors are not natural. This is also because the enforcement agency of natural flavors is the FDA and the FDA profits if the company sells more product, which is the goal of natural flavors: leaving the consumer to want more.

> There is a really interesting CBS 60 Minute segment about natural flavors: 60 Minutes-Natural Flavors

When should you buy organic?

2018

Dirty Dozen
(always buy Organic)

1. Strawberries
2. Spinach
3. Nectarines
4. Apples
5. Peaches
6. Pears
7. Cherries
8. Grapes
9. Celery
10. Tomatoes
11. Sweet Bell Peppers
12. Potatoes

Nested Blissfully

Clean 15
(OK to buy Regular)

1. Avocados
2. Sweet Corn
3. Pineapples
4. Cabbage
5. Onions
6. Sweet Peas
7. Papayas
8. Asparagus
9. Mangos
10. Eggplant
11. Honeydew
12. Kiwi
13. Cantaloupe
14. Cauliflower
15. Broccoli

These 12 fruits and vegetables are very important to buy organic because they are sprayed with the most pesticides. Pesticides are linked with many health issues that can lead to many dangerous diseases. However, if you buy organic fruit, they are not sprayed with pesticides and are very safe to eat.

Foods on the Clean 15 are very safe to buy non organic. This is because the Clean 15 list has the least amount of pesticides.

What is a Glycemic Index?

It gives you an idea about how fast your body converts the carbs in a food into glucose. Two foods with the same amount of carbohydrates can have different Glycemic Index numbers.

The smaller the number, the less impact the food has on your blood sugar.

- 55 or less = Low (good)

- 56- 69 = Medium

- 70 or higher = High (bad)

Glycemic Index

Low GI (<55), Medium GI (56-69) and High GI (70>)

Grains / Starchs		Vegetables		Fruits		Dairy		Proteins	
Rice Bran	27	Asparagus	15	Grapefruit	25	Low-Fat Yogurt	14	Peanuts	21
Bran Cereal	42	Broccoli	15	Apple	38	Plain Yogurt	14	Beans, Dried	40
Spaghetti	42	Celery	15	Peach	42	Whole Milk	27	Lentils	41
Corn, sweet	54	Cucumber	15	Orange	44	Soy Milk	30	Kidney Beans	41
Wild Rice	57	Lettuce	15	Grape	46	Fat-Free Milk	32	Split Peas	45
Sweet Potatoes	61	Peppers	15	Banana	54	Skim Milk	32	Lima Beans	46
White Rice	64	Spinach	15	Mango	56	Chocolate Milk	35	Chickpeas	47
Cous Cous	65	Tomatoes	15	Pineapple	66	Fruit Yogurt	36	Pinto Beans	55
Whole Wheat Bread	71	Chickpeas	33	Watermelon	72	Ice Cream	61	Black-Eyed Beans	59
		Cooked Carrots	39						
Muesli	80								
Baked Potatoes	85								
Oatmeal	87								
Taco Shells	97								
White Bread	100								
Bagel, White	103								

The glycemic index was developed to initially help people with diabetes and is now used to help guide consumers to eat carbohydrate-containing foods that are less likely to cause large increases in blood sugar levels. The diet could be a means to lose weight and prevent chronic diseases related to obesity such as diabetes and cardiovascular disease. There are other tools to better understand your individual diet such as the glycemic load which considers portion size and the glycemic index.

BREAKFAST

Lisa's Waffles

Why waffles? These waffles are like no other. My entire family loves these. They taste great both plain or drizzled with maple syrup. My mom and I make these at least once a week to make sure our family has a steady supply. These waffles not only taste great but they will make you feel great. Our waffles use Almond flour which is nutrient dense flour, which is good for your body and is low on the glycemic index. Unlike ordinary carbohydrates made with all purpose flour, after eating these I feel an influx of energy and sustain for a long amount of time. Normally when I eat cereal or other simple carbohydrates, that are high on the glycemic index, my body feels tired and I start getting headaches. However this never happens with these amazing almond flour waffles that my whole family enjoys. You will not be disappointed when you try this fabulous recipe for yourself.

One recipe makes 6-8 waffles (At our house we normally triple the recipe and put the extra in freezer bags to be toasted throughout the week).

Ingredients:

- 1 ½ cups almond flour
- ½ cup tapioca flour
- 1 teaspoon baking soda
- Pinch of salt
- 3 tablespoons coconut sugar
- 3 large eggs

- 3 tablespoons virgin coconut oil, warmed to liquid state
- 1 cup Califia coconut almond milk
- 1 teaspoon almond extract
- 1 teaspoon pure vanilla extract
- Canola or coconut oil spray

Directions:

1. Preheat your regular or belgium waffle maker.

2. Make the waffle batter: Whisk together the dry ingredients in a medium bowl. In a separate bowl, whisk together the wet ingredients. Add the wet ingredients to the dry ingredients and thoroughly whisk together.

3. Rest the batter: Allow the mixture to sit for 5 minutes to give the flour time to absorb the liquid.

4. Spray the waffle maker with canola oil or coconut oil to avoid the batter sticking to the waffle iron. Place the batter in the waffle maker just enough to fill the opening. Once the waffles are golden brown gently take them out of the waffle iron.

5. Enjoy your waffles and you can freeze the extra waffles in freezer bags for approximately one month.

You can use this same recipe for delicate pancakes. I like to add Lily's chocolate chips when we use this recipe for pancakes.

Breakfast Panini

Paninis are definitely not the healthiest in my book; however, it does agree with my stomach and is a simple meal no matter the time of day.

Ingredients:

- 1 tablespoon melted butter

- Bread of your choice (ezekiel, sourdough, white bread)

- Cheese of your choice (cheddar, dairy free cheese)

- Lunchmeat/ protein source (natural nitrate free ham, turkey)

- Panini maker or fry pan

Directions:

1. Lightly butter one side of 2 pieces of bread. (These will be the front and back of your sandwich)

2. Place 2-3 slices of meat and cheese inside your sandwich.

3. Place the sandwich in the panini maker until golden brown.

4. If you are using a fry pan, make sure that both sides of your sandwich are melted and golden brown.

Optional add ins: pesto, spinach, omelet or fried style egg

Mom's Banana Bread/Muffins

This banana bread is an amazing snack! For my whole freshman year and the first 3 months of my sophomore year I would almost only bring this amazing banana bread to school. Everytime I ate a piece of this delicious banana bread it felt like I was consuming a bite of goodness. Also, whenever I would bring the bread to school my friends would always bother me to have a bite because they loved the taste, but they never noticed that it had no granulated sugar and used almond flour. Along with my friends, my whole family can attest to the great taste of this recipe. Furthermore, this recipe is very fast and simple to make without a lot of effort. After eating this recipe I'm sure you will be overjoyed with the quality and taste of this recipe.

I think this recipe tastes best when kept in the refrigerator.

Yields 8 servings or 15-16 muffins

Ingredients:

- 3 large eggs
- ¼ cup oil
- ½ cup honey
- 2 bananas, mashed
- 3 cups almond flour
- ¾ teaspoon baking soda
- 1 pouch apple sauce (approximately 3 ounces)
- 2 tablespoons pure vanilla extract

Optional: 1 cup of Lily's chocolate chips or extra dark chocolate chips

Directions:

1. Preheat oven to 325 degrees Fahrenheit

2. In a large bowl, combine eggs, oil, apple sauce, vanilla and honey. Mix until well blended.

3. Add mashed bananas, almond flour and baking soda, (chocolate chips) and mix until blended.

4. Pour batter into an ungreased 8-inch square baking pan and spread evenly (or in muffin cups)

5. Bake about 40 minutes or until firm to the touch. (if using muffin cups cook for 25-30 minutes)

6. When cool, cover well. Store in an airtight container in the refrigerator for a few days or in the freezer for 2 to 3 months.

Pumpkin Chocolate Chip Muffins

Ingredients:

- 2 cups almond flour
- 3 tablespoons coconut flour
- 1 teaspoon baking soda
- 2 teaspoons cinnamon
- 1 teaspoon pumpkin spice
- ¼ teaspoon sea salt
- ¾ cup canned pumpkin
- ⅓ cup real maple syrup
- 2 large eggs
- 2 tablespoons coconut oil
- 1 teaspoon pure vanilla extract
- ½ cup Lily's chocolate chips (optional)

Directions:

1. Preheat the oven to 350 degrees.

2. Combine all the wet ingredients together (maple syrup, eggs, coconut oil and vanilla extract).

3. Add the dry ingredients and then add the Lilys chocolate chips if you decide to add chocolate chips.

4. Place paper muffin inserts into a baking tin and fill.

5. Cook for 25 minutes.

MAIN DISHES

Tasty Sweet Steak

If you need a recipe to satisfy your craving for red meat, this is the one. I love this recipe because the steak tastes juicy and sweet. No matter what quality of steak you use, this steak marinade will taste great and you will be overjoyed at the result. The steak can be paired up with any vegetable or side you enjoy. I think the steak tastes good with with a side of broccoli however it would also be great with sweet potato mash (see page 56) . Definitely give this recipe a try as it will taste great no matter what you pair it with.

Notes: I think the steak tastes best when they are cut very thin. Also, my family cooks this on the barbecue.

Ingredients:

- 1 pound lean flank steak
- 3 tablespoons coconut aminos
- 1 cup unsweetened pineapple juice
- 1 tablespoon sesame oil
- 1 clove garlic, minced
- 2 teaspoons honey
- 1 ½ teaspoons fish sauce
- ½ teaspoon freshly grated ginger

Directions:

1. Slice flank steak.

2. To create a marinade place the coconut aminos, pineapple juice, sesame oil, garlic, honey, fish sauce and ginger

3. Place the steak in a dish, pour the marinade over it, and refrigerate for 2-4 hours.

4. Preheat a grill to medium high heat

5. Cook the steak for approximately 6-8 minutes or until done.

Meatball Surprise

Yields 16 large meatballs

This recipe tastes like an authentic italian classic, however it is healthy and the whole family will enjoy it. Instead of using normal wheat flour you can use vegetable pasta. There are many different types at the market but you can get lentil pasta, zucchini and sweet potato just a few. I'm sure you will taste the superb quality and taste of this great dish.

> Sprinkle on parmesan cheese to add extra flavor

Ingredients:

- tomato sauce of your choice (2 large cans or jars)
- 3 lbs of ground turkey
- 3 eggs
- 3 cloves of garlic
- ¼ teaspoon basil
- ⅓ cup breadcrumbs or (if you want to make this recipe gluten free, instead of using breadcrumbs you can use almond flour)
- freshwater mozzarella
- parmesan cheese

Directions:

1. Mix all ingredients except for the mozzarella cheese and tomato sauce.

2. Take the turkey mixture and form a meatball, leaving indentation to put a small piece of mozzarella cheese in the center.

3. Line 1 or 2 pans with tomato sauce.

4. Place your meatballs in the pan and pour more sauce over the top of the meatballs and cook at 375 degrees fahrenheit for 45 minutes.

5. Serve with pasta. I love Cybele's vegetable pasta which comes in a variety of flavors and shapes.

Easy Teriyaki Chicken

This meal was a common one for my entire family when it became lunchtime due to its spectacular taste and simplicity. It can be made in under 10 minutes. Originally, I thought this recipe was good but quickly got bored of it and would complain that my mom made this meal too much. However, when I went on vacation with my brother and got really hungry I was actually craving some teriyaki chicken. This recipe proves a testament to the remarkable taste of this great lunch meal.

This is a very easy recipe to make quickly.

Ingredients:

- 2 lbs chicken tenders or sliced chicken

- 2 teaspoon sesame oil

- 1 cup San-J Gluten Free Teriyaki Stir-Fry & Marinade (available at Sprouts, Whole Foods, etc.)

Directions:

- Cut the chicken into small cubes, warm a large pan or stir fry pan with sesame oil.

- Cook the chicken until approximately ¾ cooked and then add 1 cup of the teriyaki sauce.

- Let the sauce cook down for approximately 5 minutes and serve with jasmine rice.

Maple Glazed Salmon

This recipe has been in the history books. Salmon is an amazingly healthy protein source and is rich in a protective antioxidant, astaxanthin, and it is an excellent source of vitamins and minerals (including potassium, selenium and vitamin B12). However, it is the content of omega-3 fatty acids in salmon that receives the most attention, and rightly so. It is this essential fat which is responsible for the reputation of oily fish as a valuable 'brain food'. These omega-3 fatty acids are a great natural addition to your diet. It helps contribute to healthy brain function, the heart, joints and general well-being. If you want a really healthy protein filled meal, pair this with the vegetable of your choice and enjoy the lasting benefits of this simple, tasty dish.

Ingredients:

- approximately 1.5-1.75 pounds of salmon cut in six pieces for six servings
- ½ cup maple syrup
- ¼ cup coconut aminos
- ¼ cup honey

Directions:

1. Line a glass baking pan with the 6 pieces of salmon evenly spread apart.
2. Mix the liquid ingredients together.
3. Bake for approximately 20 minutes at 400 degrees or until salmon is fully cooked. This salmon can also be cooked on the barbeque.
4. Serve with jasmine rice and vegetables.

Instant Pot Pressure Cooker Chicken

This recipe is a very recent addition. My family received the instant pot as a gift, however, didn't use it until the start of the March 2020 pandemic quarantine. Our favorite thing to make with the instant pot is a whole chicken. It can be cheaper than rotisserie chickens at the market and is a great meal for a big family.

This does require an Instant Pot Pressure Cooker, but it is super helpful and offers a quick way to cook chicken that is super moist and flavorful that can be used in salads, sandwiches and recipes that call for shredded and sliced chicken.

PLEASE HAVE AN ADULT ASSIST WITH THE USE OF THE INSTANT POT PRESSURE COOKER. IT IS NOT INTENDED FOR USE BY MINORS WITHOUT ASSISTANCE.

Ingredients:

- One 4-5 pounds fresh whole chicken (organic if possible)
- Pink Himalayan salt or sea salt
- One large yellow onion
- One large or 2 small lemons
- 2 cloves of garlic peeled
- Italian seasoning

Directions:

1. Gently wash the chicken and take out any loose parts. In the chest cavity insert the onion cut into quarters, the lemons cut into quarters and the peeled garlic cloves. Cover the outside of your chicken with Italian seasoning (rosemary, thyme, basil etc)

2. Place one cup of water in your Instant Pot. Place the chicken in the Instant Pot.

3. Close the Instant Pot and set for approximately 35 minutes depending on the size of your chicken.

I enjoy my chicken with sweet potatoes and brussel sprouts.

Lamb or Turkey Burgers

My family has been making lamb burgers for a while but we have just recently started adding a couple flavor packed ingredients that taste AMAZING. We started adding lemon juice, but the main new ingredient is the italian seasoning. We buy a Italian paste at Sprouts which includes (Oregano, Basil, Thyme, and Rosemary) which adds another level of flavor you will be sure to enjoy.

Ingredients:

- 3 pounds of fresh ground lamb or ground turkey
- 2 tablespoons fresh lemon juice
- ¼ cup Progresso Italian bread crumbs (this can be excluded for lamb burgers but is wonderful for turkey burgers)
- ½ teaspoon Sprouts Italian seasoning paste
- Colby jack cheese slices or dairy free cheese, as preferred

Directions:

1. Mix all the ingredients, excluding the sliced cheese. Form into approximately ¼ pound patties.
2. Put on the barbeque until fully cooked. Top with colby jack cheese or alternate.

I love these on brioche burger buns as a real treat, but you can also eat them in a pita pocket, without a bun or on gluten free bread, if you prefer.

SIDES, SNACKS AND TREATS

Steamed Broccoli

To be honest I am not a huge fan of many vegetables, but I am really trying to open myself up to trying new things and I know how important the nutrients in vegetables are to our bodies.

One vegetable that I have really grown to love is broccoli. You can get a large head of broccoli at the market or buy it from the market or cleaned and cut in bags. If you have Irritable Bowel Disease like I do it is important to cook it to make it easier to digest. I like to use a double boiler to steam the broccoli. A double boiler uses an insert to place the vegetables in that sits on top of a regular pot of steaming hot water. I like to do this for sweet potatoes, cauliflower and carrots as well.

Cook time can vary but just cook it enough to make it soft , but not mushy.

Hummus

Hummus is a perfect healthy snack. It is one of the few dips that I have greatly enjoyed since I was little and continue to enjoy it. It can be eaten with vegetables, veggies chips, Siete chips or pita bread. Hummus is so tasty no matter what you eat it with.

Ingredients:

- 1 can garbanzo beans (try to get low salt version)
- ¾ cup avocado or olive oil
- 2-3 cloves garlic
- ¼ tsp minced mint flakes (optional)
- ¼ teaspoon sea salt or pink himalyan salt
- 1 tablespoon fresh lemon juice
- 1 tablespoon tahini (if available)

Directions:

1. Drain and rinse the garbanzo beans and pat dry.
2. Put all the ingredients in a blender or food processor.
3. Blend all the ingredients.
4. You can add more oil if the consistency is too thick.

Enjoy with Siete chips or vegetable sticks.

Pearl's Thanksgiving Raspberry Cranberry Sauce

This recipe has a special place in my heart. It is simple to make and a DELI-CIOUS addition to any bird. My grandma would make this every Thanksgiving and I would enjoy it with turkey coming out of the oven. This sauce does have a lot of natural sugar, however is filled with antioxidants, which prevent cell damage or loss.

Ingredients:

- 1 bag of frozen raspberries (10 ounces)
- 1 bag of fresh or frozen cranberries (1 pound)
- 2 tart green apples peeled and cut into small little cubes
- ½ cup orange juice
- ½ cup lemon juice
- ¼ cup coconut sugar

Directions:

1. Mix the frozen raspberries, cranberries, juices and coconut sugar in a food processor.
2. After it is nice and smooth, pour into a bowl and mix in the apple cubes.
3. Refrigerate until serving.

Sweet Potato Mash

Sweet potatoes are a super easy vegetable to make and they are probably my favorite vegetable behind broccoli. Sweet potatoes are great nutritionally because they contain an array of vitamins and minerals including iron, calcium, selenium, and they're a good source of most of our B vitamins and vitamin C. One of the key nutritional benefits of sweet potato is that they're high in an antioxidant known as beta-carotene, which converts to vitamin A once consumed.

Ingredients:

- 4 large sweet potatoes
- ½ cup honey

Directions:

1. Wash and peel the sweet potatoes. Place them in a double boiler to steam until very soft.

2. Put the hot sweet potatoes in a large glass bowl and mix until smooth. Add ½ cup honey to sweeten.

For an extra treat my mom sometimes adds marshmallows that melt on the top, but this does add a lot more sugar and it isn't a clean dish, but it is yummy!

Apple Sauce

This apple sauce is very simple to make and great for any fun occasion. It is a classic recipe and is a sweet and natural way to get a sugar fix without going overboard.

Ingredients:

- 6-8 peeled granny smith apples

- 3 sticks cinnamon

- 2 cups unsweetened apple juice

Directions:

1. Cut the apples into small cubes. Place apples, cinnamon sticks and juice in a large pot.

2. Simmer for 30-45 minutes on medium heat. Stir until smooth. Refrigerate once cool.

Steve's Peanut Butter Smoothie

(Dairy free)

I named this recipe after my dad who says anything that has peanut butter in it is healthy because the peanut butter has protein in it. Obviously, this isn't fully true, but this smoothie tastes great, it is easy to make and a refreshing treat after a difficult day.

Equipment needed: blender

> If you do not have chocolate coconut almond milk you can use regular coconut almond milk or just almond milk and add chocolate syrup.

Ingredients:

- 2 cups chocolate coconut almond milk (we use Califia)

- ½ cup (dairy free) ice cream (we use Coconut Bliss' vanilla or chocolate)

- 2 cups Ice cubes

- 3 tablespoons peanut butter or almond butter (I suggest buying a peanut butter that either has one or two ingredients which should only be peanuts and it can also have salt but you don't need maple syrup or any sugar)

Directions:

1. Add all the ingredients into the blender.

2. Blend until smooth for about 1 to 2 minutes.

3. Then enjoy.

Almond Flour Chocolate Chip Cookies

We got this recipe from one of my dad's gym friends and when we tried it, we understood why it was one of her favorite recipes. I have tried many other almond and coconut flour chocolate chip cookies but this one proves superior because it doesn't bother my stomach if I have more than one cookie. This recipe is very simple to make as it only takes around 20 minutes for some fresh almond flour cookies. Whenever I make this recipe my sister is normally the most picky and won't eat some food if it is "Josh's healthy stuff" however this recipe fools her as she thinks that these are regular chocolate chip cookies, they are that good. Also if you have other people at your house you should think about doubling the recipe or else you might get sad if the cookies are eaten only a couple days or hours later.

Ingredients:

- 2 tablespoons liquid or soft coconut oil
- 3 tablespoons maple syrup
- 1 teaspoon vanilla
- 1 egg
- ½ teaspoon baking soda
- 2 cups almond flour
- ½ cup Lily's sugar free chocolate chips
- 2-3 tablespoons water (only if necessary)

Directions:

1. Put parchment paper or silicone baking mat on a cookie sheet and pre-heat oven to 375 degrees.

2. Whisk/mix the wet ingredients. Add the almond flour and then the chocolate chips.

3. The mix will be thick. If it is too thick you can add water to soften. Form the dough into balls and then flatten so they are not too thick.

4. Bake for 8-9 minutes. Recipe can be easily doubled!

Chocolate Almond Butter Bars

This is my aunt's recipe and is a great snack if you have a sweet tooth or want a nutty protein bar with 4 simple ingredients and not the long list of ingredients that many protein bars include. This recipe also takes around 10-15 minutes to prepare so if you need a refrigerator staple, this is the recipe for you. Peanut butter can also be used instead of almond butter if you do not have an allergy or sensitivity to peanut butter.

This yummy treat has two layers:

Almond Butter Base Layer:

- 1 cup natural, unsalted almond butter
- ¼ cup + 2 tablespoons pure maple syrup
- ½ cup coconut flour

Chocolate Topping Layer:

- 1 cup Lily's chocolate chips
- ½ cup natural, unsalted almond butter

Directions:

1. Line an 8x8 pan with parchment paper.

2. First, mix the almond butter base layer and place in the pan on top of the parchment paper. Smooth with a spatula or even out with another piece of parchment paper.

3. Heat the chocolate chips in the microwave in a glass bowl until the chocolate is softened and melty. Stir until smooth and add the almond butter.

4. Pour the chocolate mixture over the almond butter base layer. Even it out with a rubber spatula.

5. Freeze for 45-60 minutes or put in the refrigerator for 2-3 hours to allow to set.

6. Slice into 16 or 32 squares.

Additional Resources and References

- Dansinger, Michael. "Glycemic Index: How to Determine High vs Low Glycemic Foods." WebMD, WebMD, 16 Feb. 2019, www.webmd.com/diabetes/guide/glycemic-index-good-versus-bad-carbs.

- Leech, Joe. "11 Proven Benefits of Olive Oil." Healthline, Healthline Media, www.healthline.com/nutrition/11-proven-benefits-of-olive-oil#:~:text=Olive%20Oil%20Is%20Rich%20in%20Healthy%20Monounsaturated%20Fats&text=But%20the%20predominant%20fatty%20acid,3%20%2C%204%20%2C%205%20).

- Leech, Joe. "11 Proven Benefits of Olive Oil." Healthline, Healthline Media, www.healthline.com/nutrition/11-proven-benefits-of-olive-oil#:~:text=Olive%20Oil%20Is%20Rich%20in%20Healthy%20Monounsaturated%20Fats&text=But%20the%20predominant%20fatty%20acid,3%20%2C%204%20%2C%205%20).

- McDonell, Kayla. "8 Natural Substitutes for Sugar." Healthline, Healthline Media, 4 June 2020, www.healthline.com/nutrition/natural-sugar-substitutes#TOC_TITLE_HDR_2.

- Nutritionist, Jo Lewin - Registered, et al. "The Health Benefits of Salmon." BBC Good Food, 12 May 1970, www.bbcgoodfood.com/howto/guide/ingredient-focus-salmon.

- Palsdottir, Hrefna. "9 Evidence-Based Health Benefits of Avocado Oil." Healthline, Healthline Media, www.healthline.com/nutrition/9-avoca-do-oil-benefits#section2.

- Shubrook, Nicola. "The Health Benefits of Sweet Potato." BBC Good Food, www.bbcgoodfood.com/howto/guide/health-benefits-sweet-potato.

- Walker, Danielle, Against All Grain: Delectable Paleo Recipes to Eat Well & Feel Great. Tuttle Publishing, 2013.

Additional resources:

- YouTube - Flavcity

- YouTube - Thomas Delauer

- Ted Talk: Why we are fighting our food https://youtu.be/5-gyIkA-crM

- NPR:The invisible nutrient of the human micro biome https://youtu.be/5DTrENdWvvM

Contact me

If you have any comments or questions about the book you can email me at
cookbook.josh@gmail.com.